动物趣闻

Animal Stories

李溪 编译

版社

图书在版编目（CIP）数据

动物趣闻/李湲编译. —北京：外文出版社，2005（笑话集锦）
ISBN 7-119-04245-9

I. 动... II. 李... III. 英语-对照读物，笑话-英、汉
IV. H319.4：I

中国版本图书馆 CIP 数据核字（2005）第 111152 号

外文出版社网址：
　http://www.flp.com.cn
外文出版社电子信箱：
　info@flp.com.cn
　sales@flp.com.cn

笑话集锦
动物趣闻

编　　译　李　湲

责任编辑　李春英
封面设计　李迎迎
印刷监制　冯　浩
出版发行　外文出版社
社　　址　北京市百万庄大街 24 号　　　邮政编码　100037
电　　话　(010) 68995883（编辑部）
　　　　　(010) 68329514/68327211（推广发行部）
印　　刷　三河汇鑫印务有限公司
经　　销　新华书店/外文书店
开　　本　32 开　　　　　　　　字　　数　30 千字
印　　数　5001－10000 册　　　　印　　张　5.625
版　　次　2006 年第 1 版第 2 次印刷
装　　别　平
书　　号　ISBN 7-119-04245-9
定　　价　9.80 元

目 录
Contents

1

Parrot

鹦鹉

Never Talk to the Parrot

Mrs. Johnson phoned the repairman because her dishwasher quit working.

He couldn't accommodate her with an "afterhours" appointment and since she had to go to work, she told him, "I'll leave the key under the mat. Fix the dishwasher, leave the bill on the counter, and I'll mail you a check.

"By the way, I have a large rotweiler inside named Killer; he won't bother you. I also have a parrot, and whatever you do, do not talk to the bird!"

Well, sure enough the dog, Killer, totally

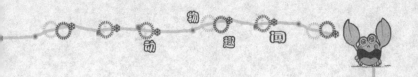

千万不要和鹦鹉说话

约翰逊太太的洗碗机坏了,她打电话叫修理工来。

他不能在下班以后来,而约翰逊太太也要上班。于是,她对他说:"我会把钥匙放在门垫下。你修好洗碗机,把账单留在餐桌上,我会把支票寄给你。"

"另外,我养了一只名叫'杀手'的大猎犬,他不会骚扰你的。我还有一只鹦鹉,你做什么都好,就是不要和它说话!"

确实,那只叫"杀手"的大狗完全不理会修理

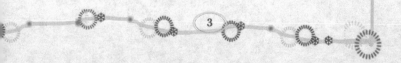

ignored the repairman, but the whole time he was there, the parrot cursed, yelled, screamed, and about did his nuts.

As he was ready to leave, he couldn't resist saying, "You stupid bird, why don't you shut up!"

To which the bird replied, "Killer, get him!!!"

工。可是，他在那儿修洗碗机时，那只鹦鹉一刻不停地咒骂、高喊、尖叫，把他烦死了。

修理工要走时，终于忍不住说道："你这只笨鸟，闭上你的鸟嘴！"

对此，鹦鹉说道："杀手，上！！！"

☆ **accommodate** /əˈkɒmədeɪt/ *v.* 使适应；使符合一致

☆ **afterhours** /ˈɑːftərˈaʊəz/ *a.* 业余时间的；在规定的打烊时间以后营业的

☆ **rottweiler** /ˈrɒtˌwaɪlə(r)/ *n.* 罗特韦尔狗（德国种黑色短毛高大猛犬）

☆ **curse** /kɜːs/ *v.* 诅咒，咒骂

☆ **yell** /jel/ *v.* 叫喊，叫嚷

☆ **drive one's nuts** 心烦意乱；发狂

He CAN Talk!

One day a man walked into an auction house. While there, he bid on a parrot.

He really wanted this bird, so he got caught up in the bidding.

He kept on bidding, but kept getting outbid, so he bid higher and higher and higher.

Finally, after he bid way more than he intended, he won the bid — the parrot was his at last!

As he was paying for the parrot, he said to the auctioneer, "I sure hope this parrot can talk. I would hate to have paid this much for it, only to find out that he can't talk!"

"Don't worry," said the auctioneer. "He can talk. Who do you think kept bidding against you?"

它会说话！

一个人走进拍卖公司。他在那儿竞拍一只鹦鹉。

他特别想要这只鹦鹉，所以他不断地出价。

他不断地出价，但总有人出价比他高，所以他的出价就越来越高。

最后，他的出价已经超出了预算。但是他竞拍成功——鹦鹉是他的了！

付钱时，他问拍卖师："我希望这只鹦鹉会说话。我可不想花了这么多钱，换回一只不会说话的！"

"不用担心，"拍卖师说，"它会说话。你以为和你竞买的是谁？"

☆ **auction** /ˈɔːkʃn/ *n.* 拍卖

☆ **bid** /bɪd/ *v.* （在拍卖等中买主）喊（价），出（价）

☆ **auctioneer** /ˌɔːkʃəˈnɪə(r)/ *n.* 拍卖商；拍卖师

The Magician and His Parrot

A young magician worked on a cruise ship with his pet parrot.

The parrot would always ruin his act by saying things like, "he has a card up his sleeve" or "he has a dove in his pocket."

One day the ship sank and the magician and the parrot found themselves alone on a lifeboat.

For a couple of days, they just sat there looking at each other.

Finally, the parrot broke the silence and said, "Okay, I give up. What did you do with the ship?"

魔术师和他的鹦鹉

一个年轻的魔术师和他的鹦鹉在一条游船上表演。

鹦鹉总是给他捣乱，说一些"他的袖子里藏了一张牌"或是"他的兜里藏了一只鸽子"之类的话。

一天，船沉了，一条救生船上只有魔术师和他的鹦鹉。

有那么几天，他们只是坐在那儿看着对方。

终于，鹦鹉打破沉默，说道："好吧，好吧，我投降。你到底对那条船做了什么？"

☆ **ruin** /'ruɪn/ *v.* 毁坏；把…无可挽回地弄糟

☆ **cruise** /kruːz/ *n.* 航行；航游

Smart Parrot

A lady walks into a pet store and asks the salesman if he has any parrots for sale.

He replies that he has a very special parrot in back.

They go to the back of the store and see a beautiful bird with a string around each leg.

The salesman explains that if she pulls the string on the left leg, the bird sings "Sunshine on My Shoulder," and if she pulls the right string, it sings "Raindrops Keep Fallin' on my Head."

The lady asks what happens if she pulls both strings, and the smart bird yells out, "Don't! I will fall on my bottom, lady!!"

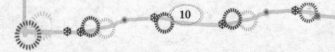

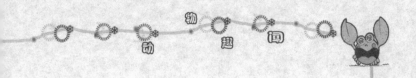

聪明的鹦鹉

一位女士走进一间宠物商店询问是否有鹦鹉出售。

店员回答说里间有一只很特别的鹦鹉。

他们走进商店的里间，看到一只美丽的鹦鹉，它的每只腿上各系了一根绳子。

店员解释说如果拉一拉鹦鹉左腿上栓的绳子，它就会唱《阳光照在我的肩膀上》；拉它右腿上的绳子，它就会唱《雨滴落在我的头上》。

女士问如果同时拉两根绳子会怎么样，这只聪明的鹦鹉叫道："千万不要！女士！我会摔个屁股蹲儿的！"

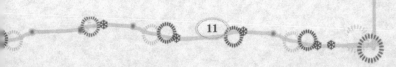

The Boss

A man goes to a pet shop to buy a parrot. The assistant takes the man to the parrot section and asks the man to choose one. The man asks, "How much is the yellow one?"

The assistant says, " $ 800 ." The man is shocked and asks the assistant why it's so expensive. The assistant explains, "This parrot is a very special one. He knows typewriting and can type really fast. "

"What about the green one?" the man asks.

The assistant says, " He costs $ 2000 because he knows typewriting and can answer incoming telephone calls and takes notes. "

老板

一个人走进宠物店要买一只鹦鹉。店员带他来到鹦鹉部让他选一只。那个人问道："那只黄色的多少钱？"

店员答道："八百元。"那个人吓了一跳，问为什么这么贵。店员解释道："这只鹦鹉非常特别，它会打字，而且打得很快。"

"那只绿色的多少钱？"那人又问。

店员答道："它要两千元，因为它不仅会打字，还能接电话并记录。"

"What about the red one?" the man asks.

The assistant says, "That one's $ 5000."

The man says, "What does HE do?"

The assistant says, "I don't know, but the other two call him boss."

"那么那只红色的呢?"

"它要五千元。"

"它会做什么?"

"我也不清楚,但是刚才的那两只都管它叫老板。"

☆ **assistant** /əˈsɪstənt/ *n.* 助手,助理

Poor Plumber

A lady was expecting the plumber; he was supposed to come at ten o'clock.

Ten o'clock came and went; no plumber; eleven o'clock, twelve o'clock, one o'clock; no plumber.

She concluded he wasn't coming, and went out to do some shopping. While she was out, the plumber arrived.

He knocked on the door; the lady's parrot said, "Who is it?" He replied, "It's the plumber."

He thought it was the lady who'd said, "Who is it?" and waited for her to come and let him in.

When this didn't happen he knocked again, and again the parrot said, "Who is it?" He said, "It's the plumber!"

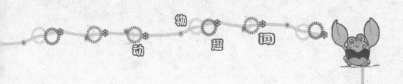

可怜的管子工

一位女士在等着管子工来，他本该 10 点来的。

10 点了，没来；11 点了，没来；12 点了，没来；1 点了，还是没来。

她认为他不会来了，就出去买东西了。她走了以后，管子工来了。

他敲了敲门，那位女士的鹦鹉说："谁呀？"他答道："我是管子工。"

他认为是那位女士在问"谁呀？"，于是就等着她来开门。

没有人来开门，他又敲了敲门。鹦鹉问道："谁呀？"他答道："我是管子工。"

He waited, and again the lady didn't come to let him in. He knocked again, and again the parrot said, "Who is it?" He said, "IT'S THE PLUMBER！！！！！！！！"

Again he waited；again she didn't come；again he knocked；again the parrot said, "Who is it?"

"Aarrrrrrgggggghhhhhhh！！！" he said, flying into a rage；he pushed the door in and ripped it off its hinges. He suffered a heart attack and he fell dead in the doorway.

The lady came home, only to see the door ripped off its hinges and a corpse lying in the doorway，"A dead body!" she exclaimed, "WHO IS IT?！"

The parrot said, "It's the plumber."

他等着，还是没有人来开门。他又敲门，鹦鹉问道："谁呀？"他答道："我是管子工！！！"

他又等着，还是没有人来开门。他再敲门，鹦鹉问道："谁呀？"

"啊——"他怒火中烧，撞进门去，把门上的合叶都撞掉了。他的心脏病发作，倒在门口，死了。

那位女士回到家，却发现门掉下来了，门口还有一具死尸。她惊叫道："一具尸体！他是谁？！"

鹦鹉答道："是管子工。"

☆ **fly into a rage** 勃然大怒，大发雷霆

☆ **rip** /rɪp/ *v.* 猛力扯掉；猛力移去

☆ **hinge** /hɪndʒ/ *n.* 铰链；合叶

☆ **corpse** /kɔːps/ *n.* 尸体

☆ **exclaim** /ɪk'skleɪm/ *v.* （由于痛苦、愤怒、激动等）呼喊，惊叫

A Burglar in Big Trouble

A burglar has just made it into the house he's intending ransacking. He shines his flashlight around, looking for valuables.

All of a sudden, a little voice pipes up, "I can see you, and so can Jesus!"

He nearly jumps out of his skin, clicks his flashlight out. When he hears nothing more after a bit, the burglar clicks the light back on and looks around the room. No one there at all, so he goes back to his business.

"I can see you, and so can Jesus!"

The burglar jumps again, he shines his light around frantically, looking for the source of the voice. Over in the corner by the window, almost

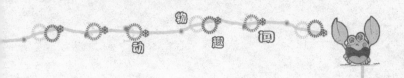

有大麻烦的盗贼

一个贼刚闯入一所房子准备行窃。他打开手电，四处找寻值钱的东西。

突然，一个微弱的声音尖声响起："我能看到你，'耶稣'也能看到你！"

贼大吃一惊，啪地关上手电。过了一会儿，他没再听到声音，就又打开手电四下看着。没有人，他又开始偷东西。

"我能看到你，'耶稣'也能看到你！"

贼又吓了一跳，他用手电四处乱照，想找到声音的来源。终于在窗角几乎被窗帘遮住的地方他看到一个笼子。笼子里有一只鹦鹉，又说道："我能

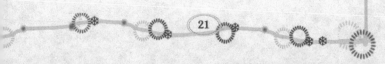

obscured by curtains, is a cage in which sits a parrot, who pipes up again, "I can see you, and so can Jesus!"

"So what," the burglar relaxes, "you're only a parrot!"

To which the parrot replies, "I'm just trying to warn you."

The burglar says, "Warn me, huh? Who in the world do you think you are? You're only a parrot!"

"Maybe, but Jesus is a rottweiler!"

看到你，'耶稣'也能看到你！"

"那又怎么样，"贼松了一口气，"你只是一只鹦鹉！"

鹦鹉答道："我只是想要警告你。"

贼说："警告我？你到底以为你是谁？你只是一只鹦鹉而已！"

"也许我只是一只鹦鹉，可是'耶稣'是一只大猎犬！"

☆ **burglar** /ˈbɜːglə(r)/ *n.* 窃贼；破门盗窃者

☆ **ransack** /ˈrænsæk/ *v.* 洗劫，把…偷窃一空

☆ **jump out of one's skin** 吓得魂灵出窍；大吃一惊

☆ **frantically** /ˈfræntɪkəlɪ/ *ad.* 发狂地；狂暴地

☆ **obscure** /əbˈskjʊə(r)/ *v.* 使变暗；遮掩，遮蔽

☆ **in the world** 究竟，到底

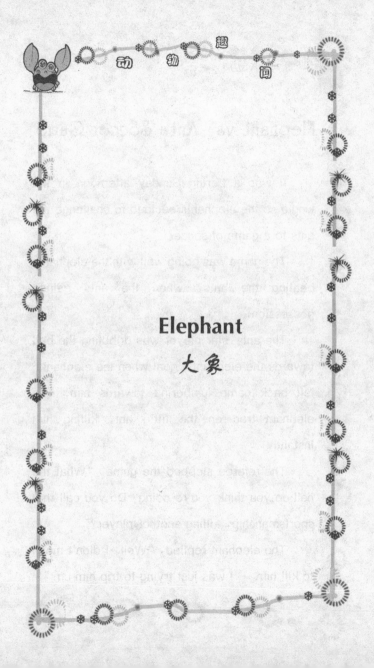

Elephant

大象

Elephant vs. Ants Soccer Game

It was a boring Sunday afternoon in the jungle so the elephants decided to challenge the ants to a game of soccer.

The game was going well with the elephants beating the ants, when the ants gained possession.

The ants' star player was dribbling the ball towards the elephants' goal when the elephants' left back came lumbering towards him. The elephant trod on the little ant, killing him instantly.

The referee stopped the game. "What the hell do you think you're doing? Do you call that sportsmanship, killing another player?"

The elephant replied, "Well, I didn't mean to kill him — I was just trying to trip him up."

大象对蚂蚁的足球赛

星期天的下午太无聊了，于是大象向蚂蚁提出踢一场足球赛。

比赛进展顺利，大象队赢球，这时，蚂蚁队控球。

蚂蚁队的明星球员将球带向大象队的球门，大象队的左后卫沉重地跑过来。它一脚踩到蚂蚁身上，当场把它踩死了。

裁判终止了比赛。"你到底在做什么？你认为杀死一名对手是体育精神吗？"

大象答道："我不是故意的，我只是想把它拌倒。"

☆ **challenge** /ˈtʃælɪndʒ/ v. 向…挑战

☆ **possession** /pəˈzeʃən/ n. 持有；拥有【体】控球权

☆ **dribble** /ˈdrɪbl/ v. 运（球）

☆ **lumbering** /ˈlʌmbərɪŋ/ a. 笨重的；动作迟缓的

☆ **trod** /trɒd/ v.（tread 的过去式）踩，踏

☆ **sportsmanship** /ˈspɔːtsmənʃɪp/ n. 公正大度的品质或精神；运动家品格

☆ **trip** /trɪp/ v. 将…拌倒，（勾脚等）使摔倒

Book About the Elephant

The French book — 1000 Ways to Cook Elephant

The English book — Elephants I Have Shot on Safari

The Welsh book — The Elephant and Its Influence on Welsh Language and Culture

The American book — How to Make Bigger and Better Elephants

The Japanese book — How to Make Smaller and Cheaper Elephants

The Greek book — How to Sell Elephants for a Lot of Money

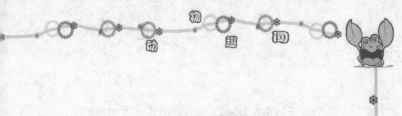

关于大象的书

法国的书——大象的一千种烹饪法

英国的书——我在东非的游猎中打到的大象

威尔士的书——大象及其对威尔士语言及文化的影响

美国的书——怎样制造更大更好的大象

日本的书——怎样制造更小更便宜的大象

希腊的书——怎样把大象卖一大笔钱

The Finnish book — What Do Elephants Think About Finnish People

The German book — A Short Introduction to Elephants, Vol. 1—6

The Icelandic book — Defrosting an Elephant

The Canadian book — Elephants: A Federal or State Issue

The Swedish book — How to Reduce Your Taxes with an Elephant

芬兰的书——大象怎么想芬兰人

德国的书——关于大象的简介，1-6卷

冰岛的书——给大象解冻

加拿大的书——大象：联邦还是国家的问题

瑞典的书——怎样用大象减税

☆ **safari** /sə'fɑːrɪ/ *n.*（东非的）（徒步）旅游；科学
   考察；游猎

☆ **defrost** /ˌdiː'frɒst/ *v.* 使解冻

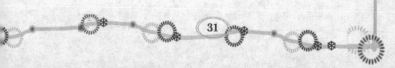

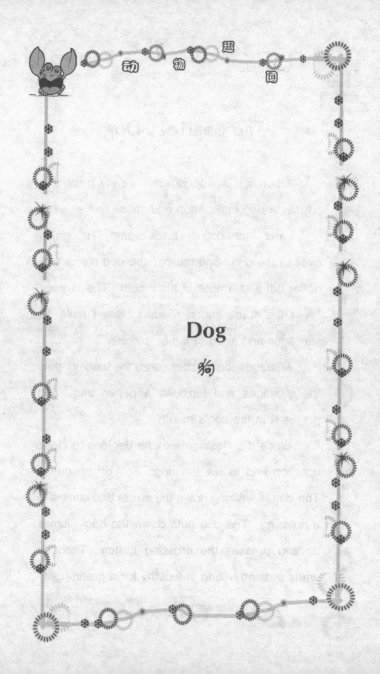

动 物 趣 闻

Dog

狗

The Smartest Dog

A butcher is working, and really busy. He notices a dog in his shop and shoos him away.

Later, the dog is back again. He walks over to the dog, and notices the dog has a ten-dollar bill and a note in his mouth. The butcher takes the note, and it reads, "Can I have 12 sausages and a leg of lamb, please."

Amazed, the butcher takes the money, puts the sausages and lamb in a paper bag, and places it in the dog's mouth.

Since it's closing time, he decides to close up shop and follow the dog. So, off he goes. The dog is walking down the street and comes to a crossing. The dog puts down the bag, jumps up and presses the crossing button. Then he waits patiently, bag in mouth, for a green light.

最聪明的狗

一个肉贩在工作，而且很忙。他发现一只狗在他的店里，就把它轰走了。

过了一会儿，那只狗又回来了。肉贩走近它，注意到它的嘴里有一张十元的钞票和一张字条。他把字条拿出来看，上面写着："请给我十二根香肠和一只羊腿。"

肉贩大为惊奇，他拿过钱，把香肠和羊腿装进一只纸袋，放到狗的嘴里。

已经到了打烊的时间，肉贩决定把店关上，跟着那只狗。于是肉贩就跟上那只狗。它沿街走到一个十字路口，放下纸袋，跳起来按行人过街灯的按

35

Then he looks both ways and trots across the road, with the butcher following.

The dog then comes to a bus stop, and checks the timetable. The butcher is in awe at this stage. The dog checks out the times, and sits on one of the seats to wait for the bus.

When a bus arrives, the dog walks to the front of the bus, looks up at the number, and goes back to his seat. Later another bus comes. Again the dog walks around to the front and looks up at the number, notices it's the right bus, and boards the bus. The butcher, by now open-mouthed, follows him onto the bus.

The bus travels through town and out to the suburbs. Eventually the dog gets up, moves to the front of the bus, and standing on his back paws, pushes the button to stop the bus. The dog gets off, groceries still in his mouth, and the butcher still following.

钮。然后它把纸袋叼在嘴里，耐心地等待绿灯。它两边看看，然后穿过马路。肉贩跟在它后面。

随后，那只狗来到一个汽车站查看时刻表。肉贩对此充满敬畏。那只狗看好时间后就坐在一张椅子上等车。

一辆车来了，那只狗走到车前，抬头看看是几路车，又走回去坐在椅子上。过了一会儿，又来了一辆车。那只狗又走到车前，抬头看看是几路车。这回是它要坐的，它上了车。肉贩看得目瞪口呆，跟着上了车。

汽车穿过城区，来到郊外。终于，那只狗起身，走到车头，用后脚撑地站起来，按下停车按钮。它叼着纸袋下了车，肉贩还跟在后面。

The dog runs up to a house. He walks up the path, and drops the groceries on the step. Then he walks back down the path, takes a big run, and throws himself — whap! — against the door. He goes back down the path, takes another run, and throws himself — whap! — against the door again!

There's no answer at the door, so the dog goes back down the path, jumps up on a wall, and walks around the garden. He gets to a window, and beats his head against it several times. He walks back, jumps off the wall, and waits at the front door. The butcher watches as a big guy opens the door, and starts laying into the dog, really cursing him.

The butcher runs up and stops the guy, "What the hell are you doing? This dog is a genius. He could be on TV, for God's sake!" To which the owner responds, "Genius, my ass. It's the second time this week he's forgotten his key!"

那只狗走向一所房子，它沿着小道走过去，把纸袋放在门前的台阶上。然后它转身走回到小道上，加速跑，"砰"的一声撞向大门。它转身走回到小道上，再次加速跑，又一次"砰"的一声撞向大门。

没有人来应门，于是那只狗又走回小道，跳上一面墙，绕过花园。它来到一扇窗下，用头撞了窗户几下。它走回来，跳下墙，在大门外等着。肉贩看到一个大个子打开门，就开始恶语相向地责骂那只狗。

肉贩跑上前去打断那个人："你在做什么？这只狗是个天才。天哪，它都可以上电视了！"狗主人答道："天才，才不呢。它这已经是这星期第二次忘带钥匙了！"

☆ awe /ɔ:/ n. 敬畏
☆ lay into 责骂，攻击
☆ curse /kɜ:s/ v. 诅咒，咒骂
☆ for God's sake [用于加强请求的语气或表示厌烦、惊奇] 看在上帝份上，做做好事吧，请帮帮忙；天哪，哎呀
☆ my ass〈美俚〉才不呢

God & Dog

On the first day of the Creation, God created the dog.

On the second day, God created man to serve the dog.

On the third day, God created all the animals of the earth to serve as potential food for the dog.

On the fourth day, God created honest toil so that man could labor for the good of the dog.

On the fifth day, God created the tennis ball so that the dog might or might not retrieve it.

On the sixth day, God created veterinary science to keep the dog healthy and the man broke.

On the seventh day, God tried to rest, but He had to walk the dog.

上帝和狗

上帝造物的第一天，造出了狗。

第二天，上帝造出了人为狗服务。

第三天，上帝造出了世界上所有的动物供狗食用。

第四天，上帝创造了诚实劳动好让人为狗的福利而努力。

第五天，上帝造出了网球好让狗自己决定要不要把它叼回来。

第六天，上帝创造了兽医学好让狗保持健康，并让人为此不断花钱。

第七天，上帝想要休息了，可是他得遛狗。

☆ **potential** /pəˈtenʃəl/ *a.* 潜在的；可能的

☆ **toil** /tɔɪl/ *n.* 长时间（或辛苦）工作，劳累

☆ **retrieve** /rɪˈtriːv/ *v.* （猎犬）衔回（被击中的猎物）

☆ **veterinary** /ˈvetərɪnəri/ *a.* 兽医的

Diagnosis Fee

A man runs into the vet's office carrying his dog, screaming for help. The vet rushes him back to an examination room and has him put his dog down on the examination table.

The vet examines the still, limp body and after a few moments tells the man that his dog, regrettably, is dead.

The man, clearly agitated and not willing to accept this, he says, "I want a second opinion."

The vet goes into the back room and brings out a cat and puts the cat down next to the dog's body. The cat walks from head to tail poking and sniffing the dog's body and finally looks at the vet and meows. The vet looks at the man and says, "I'm sorry, sir, but the cat thinks that your dog is dead too."

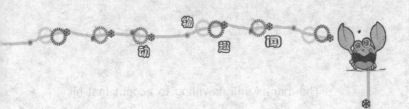

诊断费

一个人抱着他的狗跑进兽医的办公室寻求帮助。兽医马上把他带到检查室，让他把狗放在诊断台上。

兽医给这条一动不动、毫无生气的狗做了检查，遗憾地对那个人说他的狗已经死了。

那个人很焦躁，不愿意接受这个事实，他说："我要再做一次鉴定。"

兽医走入里间，抱出来一只猫，然后把猫放在狗身边。猫从头到脚地闻着、拨弄着狗的身体，最后它看着兽医喵喵叫。兽医看向那个男人说："先生，对不起，我的猫也认为你的狗已经死了。"

The man is still unwilling to accept that his dog is dead, he says, "No, I want another opinion."

So the vet brings in a black Labrador retriever. The lab sniffs the body, walks from head to tail, and finally looks at the vet and barks. The vet looks at the man and says, "I'm sorry, but the lab thinks your dog is dead too."

The man, finally resigned to the diagnosis, thanks the vet and asks how much he owes.

The vet answers, "$650."

"$650 to tell me my dog is dead?" exclaimed the man.

"Well," the vet replies, "I would only have charged you $50 for my initial diagnosis. The additional $600 was for the cat scan and lab tests."

那个人仍然不能接受这个事实，说："我要再做一次鉴定。"

兽医又带了一只黑色的拉布拉多犬出来。大犬从头到尾闻了狗的身体，最后看着兽医汪汪叫。兽医看向那个男人说："先生，对不起，我的狗也认为你的狗已经死了。"

那个人最终认了这个结果，对兽医表示了感谢，又问诊断费是多少。

兽医答道，"650 元。"

"650 元告诉我我的狗死了？"那个人大叫道。

"是这样的，"兽医答道，"我的初诊费只要 50 元，那 600 元是猫扫描和狗检查的费用。"

☆ **limp** /lɪmp/ *a.* 软弱的，无生气的，无精神的

☆ **agitated** /'ædʒɪteɪtɪd/ *a.* 激动的；焦虑的

☆ **Labrador retriever** /'læbrədɔ:(r) rɪ'tri:və(r)/ *n.* 【动】纽芬兰拾獚，拉布拉多犬（一种猎犬，为獚与谍犬的杂种，有叼物归主的习性）

☆ **resign** /rɪ'zaɪn/ *v.* 听任，顺从；辞职

Dog Property Laws

1. If I like it, it's mine.

2. If it's in my mouth, it's mine.

3. If I can take it from you, it's mine.

4. If I had it a little while ago, it's mine.

5. If I'm chewing something up, all the pieces are mine.

6. If it's mine, it must never appear to be yours anyway.

7. If it just looks like mine, it's mine.

8. If I saw it first, it's mine.

9. If you are playing with something and you put it down, it automatically becomes mine.

10. If it's broken, it's yours.

狗的财产法则

1. 我喜欢的东西，就是我的。

2. 在我嘴里的东西，就是我的。

3. 我能从你那儿拿过来的东西，就是我的。

4. 我拿了一会儿的东西，就是我的。

5. 如果我把什么东西嚼碎了，那么所有的碎片都是我的。

6. 如果什么东西是我的，那么它无论如何也不会是你的了。

7. 什么东西看上去像是我的，那它就是我的。

8. 我先看到的东西，就是我的。

9. 你在玩儿什么东西，然后又放下了，那么它自动归我了。

10. 如果什么东西坏掉了，它是你的了。

Bad Seeing-Eye Dog

A blind man is walking down the street with his seeing-eye dog one day.

They come to a busy intersection, and the dog, ignoring the high volume of traffic zooming by on the street, leads the blind man right out into the thick of traffic.

This is followed by the screech of tires and horns blaring as panicked drivers try desperately not to run the pair down.

The blind man and the dog finally reach the safety of the sidewalk on the other side of the street, and the blind man pulls a cookie out of his coat pocket, which he offers to the dog.

不称职的导盲犬

一天，一只导盲犬领着一个盲人在街上走。

他们来到一个车水马龙的十字路口。那只狗不顾路上飞驰而过的车流，将盲人直接带进车辆最密集处。

慌乱的司机们拼命地躲开他们，尖锐的刹车声和刺耳的喇叭声此起彼伏。

导盲犬终于将盲人领到马路对面的人行道上。盲人从口袋里拿出一块饼干，递给导盲犬。

A passerby, having observed the near fatal incident, can't control his amazement and commented to the blind man, "What! Your dog nearly got you killed! Why on earth are you rewarding him with a cookie?"

The blind man turns partially in his direction and replies, "To find out where his head is, so I can kick his bottom."

　　一个刚好目睹了这极其危险的一幕的路人，实在奈不住自己的惊奇，对盲人说："你在做什么！你的狗刚刚差点儿害死你！你怎么还能奖给它饼干吃？"

　　盲人转向他的方向答道："得找到它的头在哪里，我才好踢它的屁股。"

☆ **intersection** /ˌɪntəˈsekʃən/ *n.* 道路交叉口；十字路口

☆ **ignore** /ɪgˈnɔː(r)/ *v.* 不顾；不理；忽视

☆ **zoom** /zuːm/ *v.* 嗡嗡作响；隆隆地疾行

☆ **screech** /skriːtʃ/ *n.* 尖叫；尖锐刺耳的声音

☆ **blare** /bleə(r)/ *v.* 发出响而刺耳的声音

☆ **panic** /ˈpænɪk/ *v.* 使恐慌；惊慌失措

☆ **run down** （车）把…撞倒（或撞伤、撞死）

His Mother Want Him
to Be a Doctor

A guy walks into a bar with a small dog.

The bartender says, "Get out of here with that dog!"

The guy says, "But this isn't just any dog . . . this dog can play the piano!"

The bartender replies, "Well, if he can play that piano, you both can stay . . . and have a drink on the house!"

So the guy sits the dog on the piano stool, and the dog starts playing.

Ragtime, Mozart . . . and the bartender and patrons are enjoying the music.

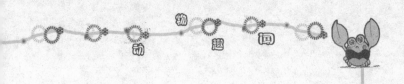

它妈妈想让它当医生

一个人带着一只小狗走进酒吧。

酒吧侍者说:"带着你的狗出去!"

那个人说:"我的狗可不是一般的狗,它会弹钢琴!"

酒吧侍者答道:"好吧,如果你的狗会弹钢琴,你们俩都可以留下,还可以免费喝酒!"

于是那个人让狗坐在钢琴凳上,开始演奏。

爵士乐、古典音乐……一曲曲演奏下来,酒吧侍者和店里的客人们都陶醉其中。

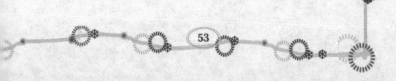

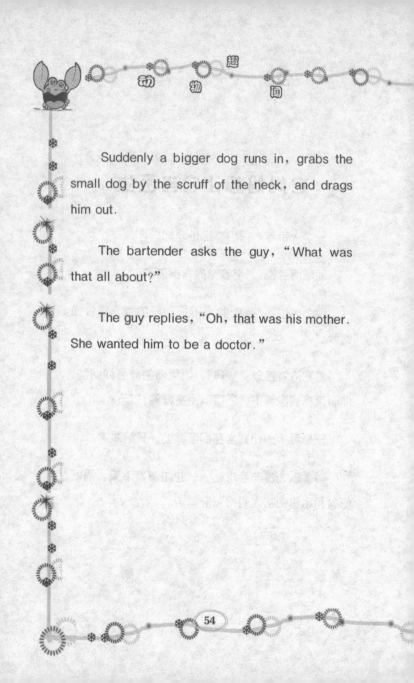

Suddenly a bigger dog runs in, grabs the small dog by the scruff of the neck, and drags him out.

The bartender asks the guy, "What was that all about?"

The guy replies, "Oh, that was his mother. She wanted him to be a doctor."

突然，一只大狗跑了进来，一把抓住小狗的后脖子，把它拖了出去。

酒吧侍者问那个人："这是怎么回事？"

那个人答道："哦，那是它妈妈。她想让它当医生。"

☆ **Ragtime** /ˈræɡtaɪm/ *n.* 【音】散拍乐，雷格泰姆（一种多用切分音法的早期爵士乐）

☆ **Mozart** 莫扎特（1756—1791），奥地利作曲家、维也纳古典乐派主要代表，5 岁开始作曲，写出大量作品，主要有歌剧《费加罗的婚礼》、《唐璜》、《魔笛》及交响曲、协奏曲、室内乐等

☆ **patron** /ˈpeɪtrən/ *n.* （商店、饭店、旅馆等的）主顾（尤指老主顾）

☆ **scruff** /skrʌf/ *n.* 颈背，后颈；颈背皮

Things Dogs Don't Understand

1. It's not a laugh to practice barking at 3 a.m.

2. It's wrong to back Grandma into a corner and guard her.

3. He shouldn't jump on your bed when he's sopping wet.

4. The cats have every right to be in the living room.

5. Barking at guests 10 minutes after they arrive is stupid.

6. Getting up does NOT mean we are going for a walk.

7. Just because I'm eating, doesn't mean you can.

狗不能理解的事情

1. 凌晨 3 点就汪汪叫不是闹着玩儿的事。

2. 把奶奶逼到角落里看着她是不对的。

3. 浑身湿透的时候不能跳到你的床上。

4. 猫可以在起居室里随心所欲。

5. 在客人进屋 10 分钟以后再冲他们叫是愚蠢的。

6. 起床了并不意味着我们要出去走走。

7. 我在吃饭并不意味着你也该吃饭了。

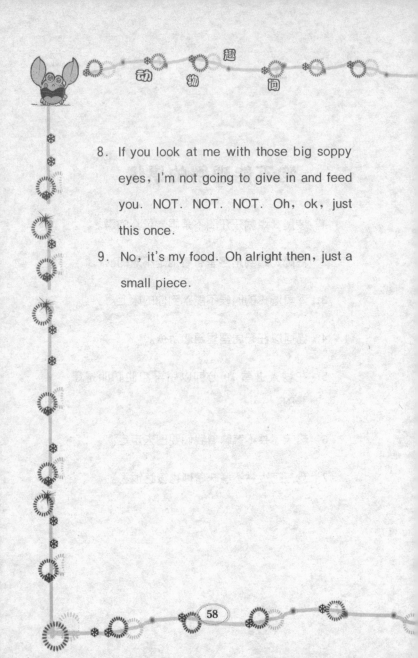

8. If you look at me with those big soppy eyes, I'm not going to give in and feed you. NOT. NOT. NOT. Oh, ok, just this once.

9. No, it's my food. Oh alright then, just a small piece.

8. 你用你那多愁善感的眼睛看着我，我也不会屈服而给你饭吃。不——不——不。哎，好吧，就这一次。

9. 不，那是我的食物。呃，好吧，就一小点儿。

☆ **sopping wet** 湿透的

☆ **soppy** /'sɒpɪ/ *a.* 湿透的；多愁善感的，易伤感落泪的

☆ **alright** /ɔːl'raɪt/ *ad.* =all right

A Talking Dog

A man and his dog walk into a bar. The man proclaims, "I'll bet you a round of drinks that my dog can talk."

Bartender: "Yeah! Sure ... go ahead."

Man: "What covers a house?"

Dog: "Roof!"*

Man: "How does sandpaper feel?"

Dog: "Rough!"*

Man: "Who was the greatest ball player of all time?"

Dog: "Ruth!"*

Man: "Pay up. I told you he could talk."

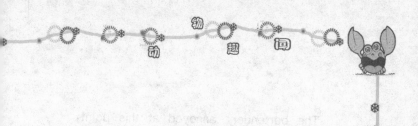

会说话的狗

一个人带着他的狗走进一家酒吧。那个人说："我跟你赌一巡酒，我的狗会说话。"

酒吧侍者："好啊，来吧。"

狗主人："房子上盖着的是什么？"

狗："汪！"（房顶）

狗主人："砂纸什么感觉？"

狗："汪！"（粗糙）

狗主人："历史上最伟大的棒球运动员是谁？"

狗："汪！"（鲁思）

狗主人："付账吧。我告诉过你它会说话。"

The bartender, annoyed at this point, throws both of them out the door.

Sitting on the sidewalk, the dog looks at the guy and says, "or is the greatest player Mantle?"

酒吧侍者到这时已经很烦他们了，于是把他们都轰了出去。

那只狗坐在人行道上，看着主人说："也许最伟大的球员是曼特尔？"

☆ **proclaim** /prəʊ'kleɪm/ *v.* 宣布，宣告；声明

☆ **round** /raʊnd/ *n.* （分发给在座者的）一份

☆ * 狗的叫声是 woof

☆ **Ruth，George Herman** 鲁思（1895—1948，美国职业棒球运动员 [1914—1935]，绰号 "Babe"，在 10 次 41 场世界联赛中创·744 的安打率最高记录，为首批入美国棒球荣誉厅的五人之一 [1936]）

☆ **Mantle，Mickey Charles** 曼特尔（1931— ，美国著名职业棒球运动员，能左右手击球，共累积打出 536 个本垒打，1969 年退出棒球活动）

A Special Dog

A woman is looking for a pet, and so she walks into a pet shop and explains her need to the attendant.

He thinks for a moment and then says, "I've got just the thing for you madam. I'll just get him."

With that, he disappears into the back of the shop, and returns a few seconds later with a cute little puppy.

"This dog is a special dog," he tells her. "It is able to fly," he explains, and with that throws the dog into the air. It immediately begins to float gracefully around the shop.

一只特别的狗

一位女士想要一只宠物，于是她走进一家宠物店并把她的需求告诉店员。

他想了一会儿说："我们这儿正好有你需要的东西，我去给你拿来。"

他走进了商店的里间，转眼又走了出来，手里拿着一只可爱的小狗。

"这只狗很特别，"他对她说。"它会飞，"他一边说，一边将小狗抛向空中。只见小狗马上开始在商店里优雅地滑翔。

"There is one problem with him, however. Whenever you say 'my', he'll eat whatever you've mentioned. Watch. My apple!"

The lady watches in astonishment as the dog zooms over to the shop attendant and furiously devours an apple he has produced from his pocket.

"He's cute, and so unusual. I'll take him," she says, and a few minutes later she is on her way back home with dog.

"Darling, look what a clever pet I bought today!" she exclaims when she gets back home. "He can fly!"

Her husband peers at the dog, and then remarks, "Fly eh? Ha! My foot!"

"但是，这只小狗也有一个问题。就是只要你说'我的'，它就会吃掉你提及的东西。看着啊——'我的苹果！'"

女士惊奇地看着小狗冲向店员，风卷残云地吞掉了他从口袋里拿出来的一只苹果。

"它很可爱，又这么不同寻常，我就要它了，"她说。几分钟之后，她就带着她的小狗在回家的路上了。

"亲爱的，看我刚买的聪明的小狗！"她进了家门就叫道："它会飞！"

她的丈夫看了看小狗，说："它会飞？哈哈！我的脚（算了吧）！"

☆ **astonishment** /ə'stɒnɪʃmənt/ *n.* 惊讶，惊愕

☆ **furiously** /'fjʊərɪəslɪ/ *ad.* 暴怒地；狂暴地；猛烈地

☆ **devour** /dɪ'vaʊə(r)/ *v.* 吞食；狼吞虎咽地吃光

☆ **peer** /pɪə(r)/ *v.* 仔细看，凝视

☆ **my foot** 〈俚语〉算了吧，去你的吧（表示不信对方的话）

Dog Rules

1. The dog is not allowed in the house.

2. Okay, the dog is allowed in the house, but only in certain rooms.

3. The dog is allowed in all rooms, but has to stay off the furniture.

4. The dog can get on the old furniture only.

5. Fine, the dog is allowed on all the furniture, but is not allowed to sleep with the humans on the bed.

6. Okay, the dog is allowed on the bed, but only by invitation.

7. The dog can sleep on the bed whenever he wants, but not under the covers.

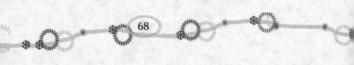

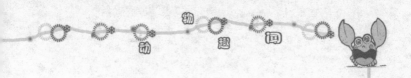

狗法则

1. 狗不能进屋。

2. 好吧，好吧，狗可以进屋，但只可以进个别房间。

3. 狗可以进所有的房间，但要与家具保持距离。

4. 狗只可以上旧家具。

5. 好吧，好吧，狗可以上所有的家具，但是不能和人一起睡在床上。

6. 好吧，好吧，狗在得到允许的情况下可以上床。

7. 只要狗愿意就可以睡在床上，但是不能盖被子。

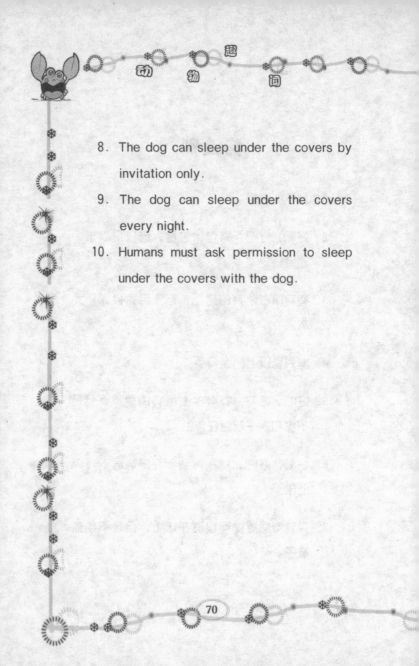

8. The dog can sleep under the covers by invitation only.

9. The dog can sleep under the covers every night.

10. Humans must ask permission to sleep under the covers with the dog.

8. 狗在得到允许的情况下可以盖被子。

9. 狗每天晚上都可以盖着被子睡。

10. 人必须要得到狗的允许才能和狗一起盖被
    子睡。

A Very Smart Dog

I went to the cinema the other day and in the front row was an old man and with him was his dog.

It was a sad funny kind of film, you know the type. In the sad part, the dog cried his eyes out, and in the funny part, the dog laughed its head off. This happened all the way through the film.

After the film had ended, I decided to go and speak to the man.

"That's the most amazing thing I've seen," I said. "That dog really seemed to enjoy the film."

The man turned to me and said, "Yeah, it is. He hated the book."

一只太聪明的狗

一天，我去电影院看电影，我的前排着一位老人和他的狗。

你知道啦，这是一部黑色喜剧片。演到伤心处，那只狗就痛哭流涕；而演到开心的地方，那只狗就狂笑不已。整个放映期间，那只狗就一直这样哭哭笑笑的。

电影结束后，我决定去和那位老人聊聊。

"这是我见过的最神奇的事情了，"我说，"您的狗看来真是很喜欢这部电影。"

老人看着我说："当然，它喜欢看电影。它讨厌看那本书。"

☆ cry one's eyes out 痛哭流涕，哭得很伤心

☆ laugh one's head off 大笑，狂笑不已

What Is a DOG?

1. Dogs spend all day sprawled on the most comfortable piece of furniture in the house.

2. They can hear a package of food opening half a block away, but don't hear you when you're in the same room.

3. They can look dumb and lovable all at the same time.

4. They growl when they are not happy.

5. When you want to play, they want to play.

6. When you want to be alone, they want to play.

7. They leave their toys everywhere.

CONCLUSION: They're tiny men in little fur coats.

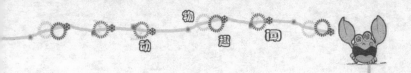

狗是什么？

1. 狗们整天整天地赖在家里最舒服的家具上。

2. 它们能听到半个街区外开食品袋的声音，
   可是你和它在同一间屋里它倒听不见。

3. 同一时间，它们能显得又笨又可爱。

4. 它们不高兴时就会乱吼。

5. 你想玩耍时，它们也想玩耍。

6. 你想一个人待着时，它们想要玩耍。

7. 它们把玩具到处乱扔。

结论：他们是披着小号毛皮外套的小号的男人。

☆ **sprawl** /sprɔːl/ v. （懒散地）伸开四肢躺（或坐）

☆ **growl** /graʊl/ v. 狂吠；发低沉的怒声；咆哮

Great Dane and Chihuahua

A man goes to a bar and he ties his Great Dane up outside.

About 10 minutes later another man comes in and asks, "Does anyone here own that Great Dane outside?"

"Yeah, I do," says the first man. "What about it?"

"Well, I think my dog has just killed him."

"What breed is your dog?"

"A Chihuahua."

"What are you talking about?! How can a Chihuahua kill a Great Dane?"

"Well, it seems he got caught in your dog's throat!!!"

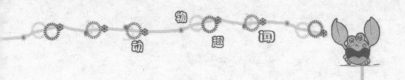
大狗和小·狗

一个人来到一家酒吧，把他的丹麦大狗栓在外面。

大约 10 分钟之后，另一个人走进酒吧，问道："门外的丹麦大狗是谁的？"

"是我的，"第一个人答道，"怎么啦？"

"呃，我的狗杀死了你的狗。"

"你的是什么狗？"

"吉娃娃。"

"你说什么？！吉娃娃怎么可能杀死大狗？"

"我想是它卡在了你的狗的喉咙里！！！"

☆ **Great Dane** 丹麦大狗（毛短而力大）

☆ **breed** /briːd/ *n.* 品种；种；属

☆ **Chihuahua** /tʃɪˈwɑːwə/ *n.* 吉娃娃（一种毛光滑的圆头小狗，原产墨西哥的奇瓦瓦）

Things Dogs Must Try
to Remember

1. The garbage collector is NOT stealing our stuff.

2. I do not need to suddenly stand straight up when I'm lying under the coffee table.

3. I will not roll my toys behind the fridge.

4. I must shake the rainwater out of my fur BEFORE entering the house.

5. I will not eat the cats' food, before or after they eat it.

6. I will stop trying to find the few remaining pieces of clean carpet in the house when I am about to throw up.

狗们一定要记住的事情

1. 收垃圾的人并不是要偷我们的东西。

2. 我趴在茶几下面的时候，完全没有必要突然站起来。

3. 我不能把玩具拱到冰箱后面。

4. 进屋之前，一定要先把身上的雨水抖干净。

5. 我既不能和猫们抢吃，也不能吃它们吃剩的食物。

6. 我要吐的时候，用不着专门去找地毯上所剩无几的干净的地方。

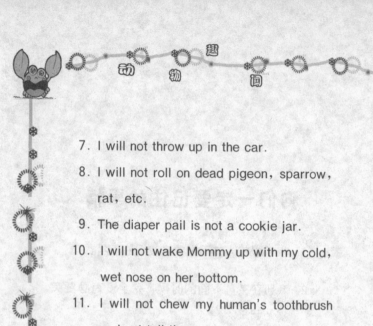

7. I will not throw up in the car.

8. I will not roll on dead pigeon, sparrow, rat, etc.

9. The diaper pail is not a cookie jar.

10. I will not wake Mommy up with my cold, wet nose on her bottom.

11. I will not chew my human's toothbrush and not tell them.

12. When in the car, I will not insist on having the window rolled down when it's raining outside.

13. We do not have a doorbell. I will not bark each time I hear one on TV.

14. I will not steal my Mom's underwear and dance all over the back yard with it.

7. 我不能在车上吐。

8. 我不能把死鸽子、麻雀和老鼠等等当玩具拨弄着玩。

9. 尿布桶不是饼干罐。

10. 我不能用我又凉又湿的鼻头贴妈妈的屁股叫她起床。

11. 我不能嚼了人们的牙刷还不告诉他们。

12. 坐车时，外面正在下雨的时候，我不能固执地要把车窗摇下来。

13. 我不能一听到电视里的门铃响就跟着叫唤，因为我们家没有门铃。

14. 我不能偷妈妈的内衣还穿着在后院里乱跑。

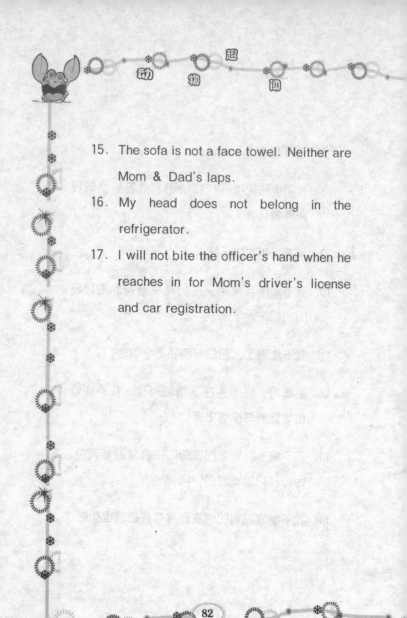

15. The sofa is not a face towel. Neither are Mom & Dad's laps.

16. My head does not belong in the refrigerator.

17. I will not bite the officer's hand when he reaches in for Mom's driver's license and car registration.

15. 沙发不是擦脸毛巾，爸爸和妈妈的衣服也不是。

16. 我的脑袋不是冰箱的一部分。

17. 警察叔叔伸手拿妈妈的驾照和行车证时，我不能去咬他的手。

☆ **throw up**〈俚语〉呕出，呕吐

☆ **diaper** /ˈdaɪəpə(r)/ *n.* 尿布

☆ **pail** /peɪl/ *n.* 桶，提桶

☆ **lap** /læp/ *n.* （人坐着时）腰以下到膝为止的大腿部；（衣服的）下摆

☆ **registration** /ˌredʒɪˈstreɪʃən/ *n.* 登记（证）；（汽车等等）执照

Bilingual Dog

A police dog responds to an ad for work with the FBI.

"Well," says the personnel director, "You'll have to meet some strict requirements. First, you must type at least 60 words per minute."

Sitting down at the typewriter, the dog types out 80 words per minute.

"Also," says the director, "You must pass a physical and complete the obstacle course."

This perfect canine specimen finishes the course in record time.

"There's one last requirement," the director continues, "you must be bilingual."

With confidence, the dog looks up at him and says, "Meow!"

能说两种语言的狗

一只警犬应征去联邦调查局工作。

"是这样的，"人事主管说，"你必须符合一些严格的要求。首先，你的打字速度要达到至少每分钟六十个字。"

那只狗坐在打字机前，打出了每分钟八十个字。

"其次，"主管接着说，"你要通过体格检查并完成障碍训练。"

这只健壮的狗以破记录的时间完成了训练。

"还有最后一项要求，"主管继续道，"你要能说两种语言。"

那只狗自信地抬起头看着他说："喵！"

☆ **physical** /ˈfɪzɪkəl/ *n.* 体格检查

☆ **canine** /ˈkeɪnaɪn/ *n.* 犬；犬科动物

☆ **specimen** /ˈspesɪmɪn/ *n.* 样本；标本；实例

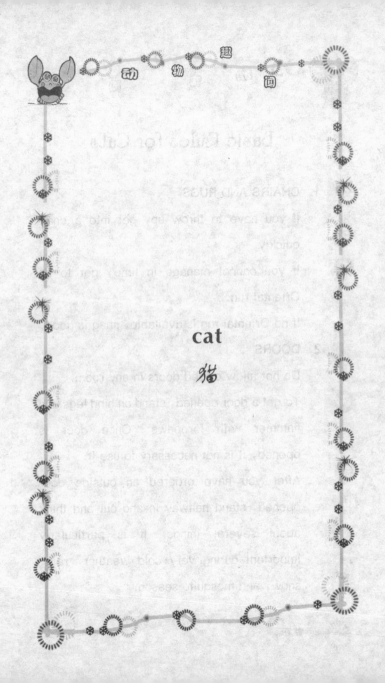

趣味动物园

cat

猫

Basic Rules for Cats

1. CHAIRS AND RUGS

If you have to throw up, get into a chair quickly.

If you cannot manage in time, get to an Oriental rug.

If no Oriental rug is available, shag is good.

2. DOORS

Do not allow closed doors in any room.

To get a door opened, stand on hind legs and hammer with forepaws. Once door is opened, it is not necessary to use it.

After you have ordered an outside door opened, stand halfway in and out and think about several things. It is particularly important during very cold weather, rain, snow, and mosquito season.

猫的基本行为准则

1. **关于椅子和地毯**

   如果要呕吐，迅速跳到一把椅子上。

   如果来不及跳到椅子上，就找一张手织东方地毯。

   如果没有手织东方地毯，长绒地毯也凑合了。

2. **关于门**

   所有房间的门都不能关着。

   叫门的方法是，用后腿支起身体，用前爪不断敲门。门开了以后就没用了。

   把户门叫开后，就不当不正地站在门中间想事情，尤其是在冷天里、下雨下雪的时候或是闹蚊虫的季节。

89

3. GUESTS

Quickly determine which guest hates cats the most. Sit on that human's lap.

For sitting on laps or rubbing against clothing, select fabric color which contrasts well with your fur. For example: white furred cats go to black wool clothing.

For the guest who claims, "I love kitties," be ready with aloof disdain; apply claws to stockings or use a quick nip on the ankle.

When walking among the dishes on the dinner table, be prepared to look surprised and hurt when scolded. The idea is to convey, "But you always allow me on the table when company isn't here."

Always accompany guests to the bathroom. It isn't necessary to do anything. Just sit and stare.

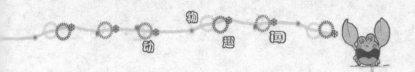

3. 关于客人

迅速判断出哪个客人最不喜欢猫，坐到他的腿上去。

找那些衣服颜色与你的毛色反差大的客人的腿上坐或身上蹭，比如：白猫找穿着黑色毛料衣服的客人。

对那些声称"我好喜欢小猫"的客人，要作冷漠的鄙视状。用爪子去钩她们的长统袜，或是在他们的脚踝上迅速咬一小口。

在餐桌上溜达时，一听到责备声，就做出一副吃惊而又无辜的样子。这样做传递出的信息是"这些人不在的时候你是让我上餐桌的"。

一定要跟着客人们去洗手间，什么事都不用做，只要坐在那儿盯着他们看就好了。

4. WORK

If one of your humans is sewing or writing and another is idle, stay with the busy one. This is called helping, otherwise known as hampering.

5. HAMPERING

When supervising cooking, sit just behind the left heel of the cook. You can't be seen and thereby stand a better chance of being stepped on, picked up and consoled.

For book readers, get in close under the chin, between the human's eyes and the book. If it is a newspaper, claw at it until shredded.

4. 关于工作

    如果你的一个主人在做针线活或写东西，而另
    一个没事做，那么要和在做事的那个待在一起，
    我们管这种行为叫帮忙。相反，和没事做的那
    个在一起叫捣乱。

5. 捣乱

    视察做饭的时候，坐在做饭人的左脚后跟处。
    在那儿你不易被发现，因此而被踩到，然后被
    抱起来抚慰。

    对于正在看书的人，爬到他的下巴处，刚好挡
    在他的眼睛和书之间。如果他看的是报纸，用
    爪子抓，直到把它抓烂。

☆ **shag** /ʃæg/ *n.* 长绒粗呢；长绒地毯

☆ **aloof** /ə'luːf/ *a.* 远离的；冷漠的；超然离群的

☆ **disdain** /dɪs'deɪn/ *n.* 鄙视，蔑视，鄙弃

☆ **convey** /kən'veɪ/ *v.* 输送；传递；表达，传达

☆ **hamper** /'hæmpə(r)/ *v.* 妨碍，阻碍；牵制

☆ **supervise** /'sjuːpəvaɪz/ *v.* 监督；管理；指导

☆ **console** /kən'səul/ *v.* 安慰，抚慰

☆ **shred** /ʃred/ *v.* 撕碎；切碎

Cat Heaven

One day a cat dies of natural causes and goes to heaven.

Greeting him the Lord says, "You've lived a good life. If there is any way I can make your stay in Heaven more comfortable, please let Me know."

The cat thinks for a minute and says, "Well, all my life I lived with a poor family and had to sleep on a hard wooden floor . . . ."

The Lord stops the cat and says, "Say no more!"

Just then a wonderful fluffy pillow appears and the cat contentedly wanders off to find a good place to nap.

A few days later six mice killed in a tragic farming accident go to heaven. The Lord is there to greet them with the same offer.

猫的天堂

一天，一只猫自然死亡，来到了天堂。

上帝在天堂迎接它，说道："过去你生活得很好，有什么方法能让你在天堂里生活得更加舒适，请告诉我。"

猫想了一会儿，说："我一直生活在一个贫穷的家庭里，我只能睡在硬木板地上……"

上帝打断猫说："不用再说了！"

猫的面前一下子出现了一只松软舒服的枕头，猫爬上去找个舒心的位置打盹。

几天后，六只老鼠在农场的一次意外中丧生，也来到了天堂。上帝迎接它们时，也问它们怎样能让它们的生活更加舒适。

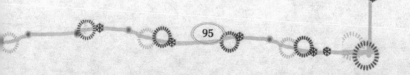

The mice answer, "All of our lives we've been chased. We've had to run from cats, from tractors, even from that farmer's wife with her broom. We're tired of running . . . ."

"Say no more!" the Lord replies.

In a flash, each mouse is fitted with a beautiful new pair of roller skates, and they skate happily off to explore the Heavenly landscape.

About a week later the Lord stops by to see the cat and finds him snoozing away. He gently wakes the cat and asks, "How are things since you got here?"

The cat stretches, yawns and replies, "Oh, it is wonderful here. I get a lot of great sleep on this pillow, and those Meals On Wheels you've been sending are the BEST!!!"

老鼠们答道:"我们的一生都在被追捕中度过。我们得避开猫、躲开拖拉机,甚至还得防着农妇的扫帚。我们跑得太累了……"

"不用再说了!"上帝说。

转眼间,每只老鼠的脚上都套上了一双崭新漂亮的滚轴溜冰鞋。它们欢快地滑走去天堂各处转悠了。

一星期后,上帝顺道去看猫,发现它在睡觉。轻轻地把它叫醒后,上帝问道:"你来天堂以后生活得怎么样啊?"

猫伸伸懒腰,打个呵欠,说道:"太棒了。我每天都在这只枕头上做很多美梦,另外,你送来的那些'轮子上的肉'是最好的美味!!!"

☆ **fluffy** /ˈflʌfɪ/ *a.* 轻软的;松软的

☆ **chase** /tʃeɪs/ *v.* 追逐;追捕

☆ **snooze** /snuːz/ *v.* 打盹,(尤指在白天)小睡

☆ **stretch** /stretʃ/ *v.* 舒展;伸直

☆ **yawn** /jɔːn/ *v.* 打呵欠

What Is a CAT?

1. Cats do what they want.
2. They rarely listen to you.
3. They're totally unpredictable.
4. When you want to play, they want to be alone.
5. When you want to be alone, they want to play.
6. They expect you to cater to their every whim.
7. They're moody.

CONCLUSION: They're tiny women in little fur coats.

猫是什么？

1. 猫们随心所欲。

2. 猫们极少听你的话。

3. 它们完全不可捉摸。

4. 你想玩耍的时候，它们想独个待着。

5. 你想一个人待着时，它们想要玩耍。

6. 它们希望你能迎合它们心血来潮的念头。

7. 它们喜怒无常。

结论：它们是披着小号毛皮外套的小号的女人。

☆ **unpredictable** /ˌʌnprɪˈdɪktəbl/ *a.* 不可预测的；不定的，易变的

☆ **cater to** 满足需要（或欲望）；投合，迎合

☆ **whim** /hwɪm/ *n.* 突然产生的念头；冲动

Is the Cat There?

A man absolutely hated his wife's cat and decided to get rid of him one day by driving him 20 blocks from his home and leaving him at the park.

As he was getting home, the cat was walking up the driveway.

The next day he decided to drive the cat 40 blocks away. He put the beast out and headed home.

Driving back up his driveway, there was the cat!

He kept taking the cat further and further and the cat would always beat him home.

猫在那儿吗？

一个人无比痛恨他妻子的猫，他决定把它处理掉。于是一天他开车来到离家二十个街区远的地方，把猫扔在了停车场。

他回到家的时候，发现那只猫正沿着门前的私家车道走来。

第二天，他决定把猫送到离家四十个街区开外的地方，他把猫扔出去后就开车回家了。

他把车开上自家车道时，发现那只猫又在那里了。

他坚持不懈地把猫送到越来越远的地方扔掉，可是猫总是能在他前面回到家。

At last he decided to drive a few miles away, turn right, then left, past the bridge, then right again and another right until he reached what he thought was a safe distance from his home and left the cat there.

Hours later the man calls home to his wife, "Honey, is the cat there?"

"Yes," the wife answers, "why do you ask?"

Frustrated, the man answered, "Put that son of a bitch on the phone, I'm lost and need directions!"

最后，他决定把猫送到更远的地方，一路上右转、左转、过桥、右转、再右转，直到他认为离家够远了，就把猫留在了那里。

几个小时后，他打电话回家问他的妻子："亲爱的，猫在家吗？"

"当然，"他妻子答道，"为什么这么问？"

那人无比懊丧地说："让那个混蛋接电话，我迷路了，需要它帮我指道！"

☆ **frustrated** /frʌˈstreɪtɪd/ *a.* 挫败的；失望的

Fly and Cat

One warm spring day, a fish was swimming about a foot below the surface of a lake and saw a fly hovering just out of striking distance.

The fish said to itself, "If that fly comes six inches closer, I'll jump up and have myself a meal."

Just then, a bear on the shore of the lake looked up and said to itself, "If that fly gets any closer to that fish, the fish will jump up, and I'll catch the fish and have myself a meal."

As luck would have it, a hunter saw what was happening. He thought to himself, "If that fly moves closer to the fish, the fish will jump, the bear will lean over to grab the fish, and I'll shoot the bear."

苍蝇和猫

一个暖洋洋的春日里，一条鱼正在湖面下一英尺处游着，它看到了一只苍蝇在它刚好够不到的地方飞。

鱼自言自语道："如果它再飞近六英寸，我就跳起来吃了它。"

这时，岸上的一只熊抬起头来自言自语道："如果那只苍蝇再飞近鱼，鱼就会跳起来吃苍蝇，我就能抓鱼吃。"

一个幸运的猎人看到这一幕，想着："如果那只苍蝇再飞近鱼，鱼就会跳起来吃苍蝇，熊就会俯身去抓鱼，我就能射熊。"

Just then, a rat was standing behind the hunter saying to itself, "If that fly moves closer to the fish, the fish will jump, the bear will lean over to grab the fish, the hunter will lean over to shoot the bear, and I'll grab the sandwich from the back pocket of the hunter."

However, unbeknownst to the rat, a cat was observing everything and thinking, "If that fly moves closer to the fish, the fish will jump, the bear will grab the fish, the hunter will shoot the bear, the rat will grab the sandwich, and I'll snatch the rat."

At that very moment, the fly dropped a few inches, the fish grabbed the fly, the bear grabbed the fish, the hunter shot the bear, the rat grabbed the sandwich, the cat jumped, missed the rat and landed in the lake.

这时，一只站在猎人身后的老鼠自言自语道："如果那只苍蝇再飞近鱼，鱼就会跳起来吃苍蝇，熊就会俯身去抓鱼，猎人就会弓身射熊，我就能从猎人的后兜里偷出三明治吃。"

然而，老鼠不知道的是，一只猫看到了一切，它在想："如果那只苍蝇再飞近鱼，鱼就会跳起来吃苍蝇，熊就会俯身去抓鱼，猎人就会弓身射熊，老鼠就会从猎人的后兜里偷三明治，我就能趁机抓住老鼠。"

就在这时，苍蝇往下飞了几英寸，鱼抓到了苍蝇，熊抓到了鱼，猎人射中了熊，老鼠偷到了三明治，猫跳了起来，没有扑到老鼠，掉进了湖里。

☆ **hover** /ˈhɒvə(r)/ *v.* 翱翔，盘旋

☆ **striking distance** 攻击距离

☆ **unbeknownst** /ˌʌnbɪˈnəʊnst/ *a.* 〈口〉未知的；不为人所知的

☆ **snatch** /snætʃ/ *v.* 夺；一把抓住；抓住机会做

动物 趣闻

horse

马

Blind Benny

An out-of-towner accidentally drives his car into a deep ditch on the side of a country road. Luckily a farmer happened by with his big old horse named Benny.

The man asked for help. The farmer said Benny could pull his car out. So he backed Benny up and hitched Benny to the man's car bumper.

Then he yelled, "Pull, Nellie, pull."

Benny didn't move.

Then he yelled, "Come on, pull Ranger."

Still, Benny didn't move.

Then he yelled really loud, "Now pull, Fred, pull hard."

瞎本尼

一个外地人在乡村公路上开车时不小心开到了路边的沟渠里。幸运的是正巧有个农夫牵着他高大的老马从旁经过。

外地人向他求助。农夫说他的马本尼能把车拉出来。他让马后退几步,拴在车的保险杠上。

然后,农夫喊道:"拉,内莉,拉啊。"

本尼没动。

农夫又喊道:"来啊,拉,兰格。"

本尼还是没动。

农夫再次大声叫道:"拉呀,弗雷德,使劲拉。"

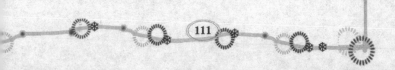

Benny just stood.

Then the farmer nonchalantly said, "Okay, Benny, pull."

Benny pulled the car out of the ditch.

The man was very appreciative but curious. He asked the farmer why he called his horse by the wrong name three times.

The farmer said, "Oh, Benny is blind, and if he thought he was the only one pulling he wouldn't even try."

本尼站着一动不动。

最后，农夫淡淡地说："好啦，本尼，拉吧。"

本尼把车从沟渠里拉了出来。

外地人非常感激农夫，但是对农夫的做法很好奇。他问农夫为什么三次叫错马的名字。

农夫说："是这样的，本尼的眼睛瞎了，如果它认为只有它自己在拉车，那它根本就不会卖力尝试的。"

☆ **hitch** /hɪtʃ/ *v.* 钩住；拴住；系住；套住

☆ **bumper** /ˈbʌmpə(r)/ *n.* （汽车的）保险杠

☆ **nonchalantly** /ˈnɒnʃələntlɪ/ *ad.* 漠不关心地

☆ **appreciative** /əˈpriːʃɪətɪv/ *a.* 表示赞赏的；感激的

Race Records

Some race horses staying in a stable. One of them starts to boast about his track record.

"In the last 15 races, I've won 8 of them!"

Another horse breaks in, "Well, in the last 27 races, I've won 19!!"

"Oh that's good, but in the last 36 races, I've won 28!" says another, flicking his tail.

At this point, they notice that a greyhound dog has been sitting there listening.

"I don't mean to boast," says the greyhound, "but in my last 90 races, I've won 88 of them!"

The horses are clearly amazed.

"Wow!" says one, after a hushed silence. "A talking dog."

赛跑记录

几匹赛马在马厩里，其中一匹开始吹嘘自己的赛绩。

"在过去的十五场马赛中，我赢了八场！"

另一匹马插进来说："在过去的二十七场中我赢了十九场！！"

"哦，还不错，不过在过去的三十六场中，我赢了二十八场！"又一匹赛马呼扇着尾巴，加进来说道。

这时，它们注意到一只猎犬坐在那儿听它们说话。

"我可不是吹牛，"猎犬说，"在我参加过的九十场比赛中，我赢了八十八场！"

马们显而易见地很吃惊。

"哇！"一匹马在一阵死寂后说，"一只会说话的狗。"

☆ **greyhound** /ˈgreɪhaʊnd/ *n.* 灵猩（一种身细腿长的猎犬）

☆ **hushed** /hʌʃt/ *a.* 寂静的；秘密的

☆ **talking** /ˈtɔːkɪŋ/ *a.* 说话的；会学人语的；多嘴的

Horse and His Own Pear

A sparrow is chirping in a tree in the woods when a horse walks up and sits on the tree root.

"What are you doing here?" asks the sparrow.

"I'm here to eat some pear."

"But this is a pine tree!"

"I know. I brought my own pear."

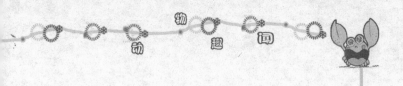

马和它自己的梨

树林里，一只麻雀正在树上喳喳叫。这时，一匹马走过来坐在树下。

"你来这里做什么？"麻雀问道。

"我来吃梨。"

"可这是一棵松树！"

"我知道，我自己带了梨来。"

☆ chirp /tʃɜːp/ v. 啁啾；唧唧叫

Other Animals

其它动物

Two Bats

Two vampire bats wake up in the middle of the night, thirsty for blood. One says, "Lets fly out of the cave and get some blood."

"We're new here," says the second one. "It's dark out, and we don't know where to look. We'd better wait until the other bats go with us."

The first bat replies, "Who needs them? I can find some blood somewhere."

He flies out of the cave.

When he returns, he is covered with blood.

The second bat says excitedly, "Where did you get the blood?"

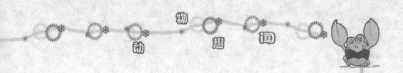

两只蝙蝠

两只吸血蝙蝠在半夜醒来，想要喝血。一只蝙蝠说："我们飞到洞外去找些血喝。"

"我们是新来的，"另一只说，"外面太黑了，我们不知道到哪儿去找。还是等其它蝙蝠带我们一起去吧。"

第一只蝙蝠答道："谁需要它们？我能找到血。"

它飞出洞去。

它回来的时候浑身是血。

另一只蝙蝠兴奋地问："你从哪儿弄到的血？"

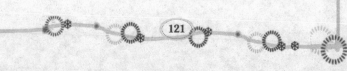

The first bat takes his buddy to the mouth of the cave. Pointing into the night, he asks, "See that black building over there?"

"Yes," the other bat answers.

"Well," says the first bat, "I didn't."

第一只蝙蝠把同伴带到洞口，指向茫茫夜色，问道："你看到那边那栋黑色的建筑了吗?"

"看到了，"另一只蝙蝠答道。

"可是，"第一只蝙蝠说，"我没看见。"

☆ vampire /'væmpaɪə(r)/ n. 吸血鬼;【动】吸血蝙
蝠

☆ thirsty /'θɜːstɪ/ a. 渴的；渴望的，渴求的

☆ buddy /'bʌdɪ/ n.〈口〉好朋友，同志，伙伴

Three Tough Mice

Three rats are sitting at the bar bragging about their bravery and toughness.

The first says, "I'm so tough, once I ate a whole bagful of rat poison!"

The second says, "Well I'm so tough, once I was caught in a rat trap and I bit it apart!"

Then the third rat gets up and says, "Later guys, I'm off home to harass the cat."

三只坚强的老鼠

三只老鼠坐在酒吧里互相吹嘘自己的勇敢和强壮。

第一只说："我很强壮，有一次我吃了一整袋的老鼠药！"

第二只说："还是我强壮，有一次我被老鼠夹夹住，可是我把它咬开了！"

第三只老鼠站起来说："伙计们，我这就要回家逗猫去了。"

☆ **brag** /bræg/ *v.* 自夸，吹嘘

☆ **harass** /ˈhærəs/ *v.* 不断侵扰，骚扰，扰乱

Poor Baby Turtle

Deep within a forest, a baby turtle was standing at the bottom of a large tree and with a deep sigh, started to climb.

After hours of effort, he reached a very high branch and walked along to the end. He turned and spread all four flippers and jumped into the air.

On landing at the bottom in a pile of soft, dead leaves, he shook himself off, walked back to the bottom of the tree and with a sigh started to climb.

Hours later, he again reached the very high branch, walked along, turned, spread his flippers and launched himself off the branch.

126

可怜的小乌龟

森林深处，一只小乌龟站在一棵大树脚下。它深深地叹了一口气，开始往上爬。

几个小时后，它终于爬到了一根很高的树杈上，沿着树枝走到尽头。它转过身，伸展四肢，跳了出去。

掉到树下一堆松软的枯叶中，它抖了抖身子，走回到大树脚下，叹了一口气，又开始往上爬。

几个小时过去了，它又爬到那根高高的树杈上，走到尽头，转身，伸展四肢，跳了出去。

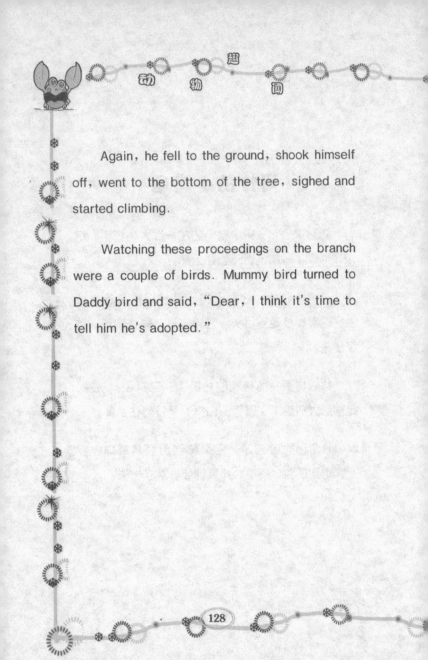

Again, he fell to the ground, shook himself off, went to the bottom of the tree, sighed and started climbing.

Watching these proceedings on the branch were a couple of birds. Mummy bird turned to Daddy bird and said, "Dear, I think it's time to tell him he's adopted."

它再一次掉到地上，抖了抖身子，走回到大树脚下，叹了一口气，再一次开始往上爬。

一对鸟夫妻站在树枝上看着小乌龟。鸟妈妈转头对鸟爸爸说："亲爱的，我想我们该告诉它它是我们收养的孩子了。"

☆ **flipper** /ˈflɪpə(r)/ *n.*（鲸、海豹、海龟等的）鳍（状）肢，前肢，鳍足

☆ **launch** /lɔːntʃ/ *v.* 投射；投出

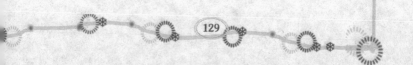

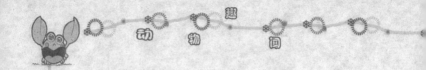

The Snakes

There were two snakes talking in the bush.

The first one said, "Are we the type of snakes who wrap ourselves around our prey and squeeze and crush until they're dead? Or are we the type of snake who ambush our prey and bite them and they are poisoned?"

Then the second snake says, "Why do you ask?"

The first one replies, "I just bit my lip!"

蛇

树丛里有两只蛇在交谈。

第一只说："我们是那种缠住我们的猎物把它们挤死的蛇，还是那种伏击猎物，然后咬它们，把它们毒死的蛇呢？"

另一只蛇说："你为什么这么问？"

第一只蛇说："我刚咬到了自己的嘴唇！"

☆ **wrap** /ræp/ *v.* 包；裹；缠绕

☆ **prey** /preɪ/ *n.* 被捕食的动物，捕获物

☆ **squeeze** /skwiːz/ *v* 榨取；用力挤压

☆ **crush** /krʌʃ/ *v.* 压碎；压伤；紧抱

☆ **ambush** /ˈæmbʊʃ/ *v.* 埋伏；伏击

King of the Jungle

A lion woke up one morning in the jungle.

He went out and cornered a small monkey and roared, "Who is mightiest of all jungle animals?"

The trembling monkey says, "You are, mighty lion!"

Later, the lion confronts a ox and fiercely bellows, "Who is the mightiest of all jungle animals?"

The terrified ox stammers, "Oh great lion, you are the mightiest animal in the jungle!"

On a roll now, the lion swaggers up to an elephant and roars, "Who is mightiest of all jungle animals?"

森林之王

丛林里一只狮子在早上醒来。

它走出去，逼住一只小猴子吼道："谁是丛林中最强大的动物？"

小猴子哆哩哆嗦地答道："是您，伟大的狮子！"

一会儿，狮子又遇到一头牛，它狂暴地吼道："谁是丛林中最强大的动物？"

牛吓坏了，结结巴巴地答道："啊，伟大的狮子，您是丛林中最强大的动物！"

狮子得意忘形了，它大摇大摆地走到一头大象跟前吼道："谁是丛林中最强大的动物？"

Fast as lightning, the elephant snatches up the lion with his trunk, slams him against a tree half a dozen times leaving the lion feeling like it'd been run over by a tractor.

The elephant then stomps on the lion till it looks like a corn tortilla and ambles away.

The lion lets out a moan of pain, lifts his head weakly and hollers after the elephant, "Just because you don't know the answer, you don't have to get so upset about it!"

大象飞快地用鼻子抓过狮子，把它甩到一棵树上撞了几次。狮子感觉就好像被拖拉机碾过一样。

大象又在狮子身上踩了几下，把它踩扁在地，然后踱着步子走开了。

狮子痛苦地呻吟着，虚弱地抬起头，对着大象叫道："就算你不知道答案，也用不着这么烦躁嘛！"

☆ **corner** /'kɔːnə(r)/ v. 使陷入困境

☆ **confront** /kən'frʌnt/ v. 迎面遇到；面临；遭遇

☆ **bellow** /'beləʊ/ v. 怒吼，咆哮

☆ **stammer** /'stæmə(r)/ v. 结结巴巴地说，口吃

☆ **on a roll** 连连获胜中；连续交好运中

☆ **swagger** /'swægə(r)/ v. 昂首阔步；大摇大摆地走

☆ **snatch** /snætʃ/ v. 一下子拉；一把抓住

☆ **slam** /slæm/ v. 使劲扔；使劲推；猛击

☆ **stomp** /stɒmp/ v. 踩脚；重踩，重踏

☆ **tortilla** /tɔː'tɪlə/ n. 玉米粉圆饼

☆ **amble** /'æmbl/ v. 缓行；轻松地走，从容漫步

☆ **holler** /'hɒlə(r)/ v. 叫喊，嚷嚷

The Koala Bear

A koala bear walks into a bar, sits down and tells the bartender that he wants to have lunch.

The bartender gives him a menu and he orders a sandwich.

The koala eats the sandwich, and when he finishes, he gets up to leave. Suddenly, he pulls a pistol out of his pouch, shoots the bar to pieces, and proceeds to walk out of the bar.

The bartender, in shock, shouts to the koala, "hey who do you think you are, you ate my sandwich and shot up my bar, and now you are just going to leave!"

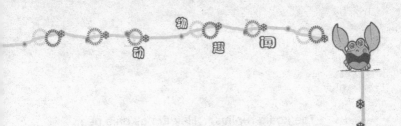
树袋熊

一只树袋熊走进一家餐吧，坐下说它要吃午饭。

侍者把餐单递给它，它点了一份三明治。

树袋熊吃完三明治，起身往外走。突然，它从育儿袋里抽出一支枪，把餐吧里打得七零八落，然后走了出去。

侍者震惊地冲它叫道："你以为你是谁呀，你吃了我的三明治，又把我的餐吧打得乱七八糟，你竟然就要走了！"

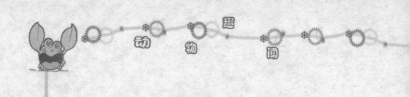

The koala replies, "Hey I'm a koala bear."

The bartender says, "Yeah, so?"

The koala bear replies, "Look it up."

The frustrated bartender pulls out his encyclopedia from behind the ruined bar and looks up "koala", and sure enough, there is a picture of the koala bear.

He reads the caption, which says, "a marsupial that eats shoots and leaves."

树袋熊答道："我是树袋熊。"

侍者说："那又怎么样？"

树袋熊说："去查查吧。"

沮丧的侍者从毁损的餐吧里找出百科全书，查到"树袋熊"，当然，书上有一张树袋熊的图片。

他看向图片下面的说明文字，上面写着："一种吃完、射击后离去的有袋目动物（一种以嫩枝和树叶为食的有袋目动物）。"

☆ **pouch** /pautʃ/ *n.* （随身携带的）小袋；（袋鼠等有袋目动物腹部的）育儿袋

☆ **marsupial** /mɑːˈsjuːpiəl/ *n.* 【动】有袋（目）动物

☆ **caption** /ˈkæpʃən/ *n.* （图片的）说明文字；（影片的）字幕；（章节、诗歌等的）标题

☆ **shoot** /ʃuːt/ *n.* 芽；苗；嫩枝
　　　　　　　v. 射击；射伤；摧毁

☆ **leaves** /liːvz/ *n.* leaf（树叶）的复数
　　　　　　　v. leave（离去）的第三人称单数

If You Are Warm and Happy

Once upon a time, there was a nonconforming sparrow who decided not to fly south for the winter.

He said, "I've had enough of this flying south every winter, I'll just stay right here on this farm, what's the big deal, anyway?"

However, soon winter came and the weather turned so cold that he was afraid that he might freeze to death. So he reluctantly started to fly south.

In a short time, ice began to form on his wings and he fell to earth in a barnyard, almost frozen.

The poor bird was cold, tired and hungry. "Why did I stay?" he asked himself.

A cow passed by and crapped on the little sparrow. The crap was too heavy for the spar-

如果你温暖而快乐

从前，一只不守常规的麻雀决定冬天的时候不飞去南方。

它说："每年冬天都飞去南方，我受够了。这回我就要留在这儿，在这个农场里过冬，有什么大不了的？"

然而不久，冬天就来了，天气很冷，麻雀担心自己会被冻死。于是它不情不愿地向南方飞去。

飞不多久，它的翅膀上就结冰了。麻雀掉到一个谷仓旁的场地上，几乎冻僵了。

这可怜的小鸟饥寒交迫，而且累坏了，它问自己："我为什么要留下来呢？"

一头牛路过这里，还在小麻雀的身上拉了好大一泡屎。小麻雀钻不出来，它想自己死到临头了。可没想到，热热的牛屎温暖了它，它翅膀上的冰化了。

141

row to free himself and he thought it was the end. But, the manure warmed him and defrosted his wings.

Warm and happy, able to breathe, he started to sing. Just then a large cat came by and, hearing the chirping, went down to investigate the sounds.

The cat cleared away the manure, found the chirping bird. The sparrow was so happy to be free from the crap that he thanked the cat who promptly ate him.

The moral of the story:

1. Just because someone craps on you, it does not make him your enemy.

2. Just because someone gets you out of the crap, it does not make him your friend.

3. And, if you're warm and happy in a pile of crap, keep your mouth shut.

温暖而快乐的小麻雀一能呼吸就开始唱歌。就在这时，一只大猫经过这里，听到了小麻雀的叫声，循声找了过来。

猫清走了牛屎，发现了唧唧喳喳的小麻雀。小麻雀重获自由太高兴了，它谢了猫。而猫——马上把它吃掉了。

这个故事的寓意是：

有人只是在你身上拉屎并不意味着他是你的敌人。

有人把你从屎里救出来并不意味着他就是你的朋友。

如果你在一堆屎里感到温暖而快乐，记得把嘴闭上。

☆ **nonconforming** /ˌnɒnkənˈfɔːmɪŋ/ *a.* 不一致的，不符合的；不从国教的

☆ **big deal** ［常用作反语］至关重要的大事，了不得的事情

☆ **reluctantly** /rɪˈlʌktəntlɪ/ *ad.* 不情愿地；勉强地

☆ **crap** /kræp/ *v.* 〈粗〉拉屎；〈口〉胡扯

☆ **manure** /məˈnjʊə(r)/ *n.* 肥料；粪肥

☆ **defrost** /ˌdiːˈfrɒst/ *v.* 除去…的冰霜；使解冻

Four Monkeys in a Tree

There were 4 monkeys in a tree.

Why did the first monkey fall out of the tree?

— It died.

Why did the second monkey fall out of the tree?

— It was tied on to the first monkey.

Why did the third monkey fall out of the tree?

— It got hit by the first two.

Why did the fourth monkey fall out of the tree?

— Peer pressure.

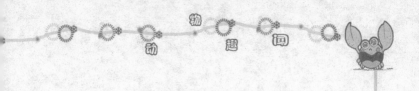
树上的四只猴子

树上有四只猴子。

为什么第一只猴子从树上掉了下来？

——因为它死了。

——为什么第二只猴子从树上掉了下来？

——因为它和第一只猴子拴在一起了。

——为什么第三只猴子从树上掉了下来？

——它是被前两只猴子撞下来的。

为什么第四只猴子从树上掉了下来？

——从众心理。

A Turkey's Tragedy

Chatting with a bull, a turkey sighed and said, "I would love to be able to get to the top of that tree, but I haven't got the energy."

"Well, why don't you nibble on some of my droppings?" replied the bull. "They're packed with nutrients."

The turkey pecked at a lump of dung and found that it actually gave him enough strength to reach the first branch of the tree.

The next day, after eating some more dung, the turkey reached the second branch.

Finally, after a week, there he was, proudly perched at the top of the tree.

火鸡的悲剧

一只火鸡在和一头公牛聊天时叹着气说道："我想飞到那棵树顶上去，可是我没那份力气。"

"这样啊，你干吗不吃点儿我的粪便呢？"公牛答道，"很有营养。"

火鸡吃了一点后，发现自己真的有力气飞上那棵树最矮的枝杈。

第二天，又吃了一些牛粪后，火鸡飞上了高一层的枝杈。

终于，在一个星期后，火鸡骄傲地飞上了那棵树的顶端。

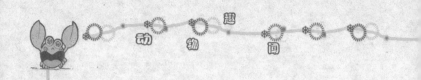

Soon, though, the turkey was promptly spotted by a hunter who shot the turkey from the tree.

The moral of the story is:

Bullshit might get you to the top, but it won't keep you there.

然而，火鸡马上就被猎人发现后打了下来。

这个故事的寓意是：

牛屎（吹牛）也许能让你爬上去，却不能让你在上面待稳。

☆ **nibble** /'nɪbl/ v. 啃；一点一点地咬（或吃）

☆ **droppings** /'drɒpɪŋz/ n. （兽、鸟等的）粪

☆ **nutrient** /'njuːtrɪənt/ n. 营养品，滋养物；食物

☆ **peck** /pek/ v. 啄食

☆ **perch** /pɜːtʃ/ v. 飞落，暂栖

☆ **bullshit** /'bʊlʃɪt/ n.〈粗〉胡说；废话；大话

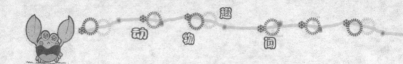

Duck Who Loves Grapes

A duck walks into a convenience store on Wednesday afternoon. He asks the storeowner if they have any grapes for sale.

The storeowner says, "No. But we'll get some in on Monday."

Duck says, "Okay." and he leaves.

On Thursday, the duck comes back in and says, "You got any grapes?"

The owner once again replies, "I told you yesterday, and I'll tell you today: We don't get any grapes in until next Monday!"

The duck says, "Okay." and he leaves.

On Friday, the duck walks in again and asks, "You got any grapes?"

爱吃葡萄的鸭子

星期三的下午，一只鸭子走进一间便利店。它问店主有没有葡萄卖。

店主答道："现在没有。但是我们星期一会进一些。"

鸭子说："好吧。"就走了。

星期四，鸭子又走进店来问："有葡萄吗?"

店主又答道："昨天我就告诉你了，今天我再说一遍：我们下星期一才会进葡萄。"

鸭子说："好吧。"就走了。

星期五，鸭子又走进店来问："有葡萄吗?"

The owner is very annoyed and screams at him, "LOOK! I told you yesterday, I told you the day before yesterday, and I'll tell you today, WE DON'T GET ANY GRAPES IN UNTIL NEXT MONDAY!! If you come in here again and ask for grapes before Monday, I'm gonna nail your bill to the floor!"

The duck replies, "Okay," and leaves.

On Saturday, the duck returns once again and asks, "You got any nails?"

The owner says, "No."

The duck says, "Well then, you got any grapes?"

店主不胜其烦地冲它大叫："你听好喽！我前天就告诉你了，我昨天也告诉你了，我今天再说一遍，我们下星期一才会进葡萄！！如果你在下星期一之前再进来问我要葡萄，我就用钉子把你的大嘴钉在地上。"

鸭子说："好吧。"就走了。

星期六，鸭子又来了，问道："有钉子吗？"

店主说："没有。"

鸭子说："好吧，有葡萄吗？"

☆ **convenience** /kən'vi:njəns/ *n.* 方便；舒适；便利设施

☆ **scream** /skri:m/ *v.* 尖声喊叫；歇斯底里地叫喊

Poor Frog

A lonely frog telephoned the Psychic Hotline and asked what his future holds.

His Personal Psychic Advisor tells him, "You are going to meet a beautiful young girl who will want to know everything about you."

The frog is thrilled, "This is great!"

"Will I meet her at a party?" he croaks.

"No," says the psychic advisor, "in biology class."

可怜的青蛙

一只孤独的青蛙打电话给心灵热线问自己的将来。

它的私人顾问对它说:"你会遇到一个漂亮的小姑娘,她会想要全方位地了解你。"

青蛙激动地说:"这太棒了!"

"我是在晚会上认识她的吗?"青蛙呱呱叫着。

"不是,"顾问说,"是在生物课上。"

☆ **psychic** /'saɪkɪk/ *a.* 精神的,心灵的;超自然的

☆ **thrill** /θrɪl/ *v.* 非常激动,非常兴奋;颤抖

Poor Snake

An old snake goes to see his doctor.

"Doctor, I need something for my eyes, I can't see very well these days."

The doctor fixes him up with a pair of glasses and tells him to return in 2 weeks.

The snake comes back in 2 weeks and tells the doctor he's very depressed.

The doctor says, "What's the problem? Didn't the glasses help you?"

"The glasses are fine doctor, but I just discovered I've been living with a water hose the past 2 years!"

可怜的蛇

一只上了年纪的蛇去看医生。

"医生，我该配副眼镜了，这段日子以来我一直看不清东西。"

医生给它配了一副眼镜，并让他两个星期后来复查。

两个星期后，老蛇又来了，它对医生说它很郁闷。

医生问："怎么啦？眼镜的度数不对吗？"

"眼镜很好，医生，只是我才发现我和一根水管一起生活了两年！"

☆ depressed /dɪ'prest/ *a.* 抑郁的，沮丧的

☆ hose /həuz/ *n.* 软管；水龙带

Christian Bear

One day this preacher decided that he would skip church and go hunting.

When in the woods he came upon a bear. He started running, and he ran for a while until all of a sudden he tripped over a tree root. At this moment he was almost face to face with the bear.

He dropped to his knees and said, "Dear Lord, if there is one wish I would want for you to give me it would be to make this bear a Christian."

And at that instant, he bear halted to a stop and dropped to his knees and said, "Dear Lord, thank you for the food I am about to receive!"

基督徒熊

一天，牧师决定不去教堂而去打猎。

在丛林中他遇到了一只熊。他开始跑，跑啊跑，突然他被树根绊倒了。熊就近在眼前了。

他跪倒在地，说道："上帝，我祈祷这只熊是个基督徒。"

就在这时，那只熊停下脚步，跪了下来说："上帝，感谢你赐予我的食物！"

☆ **skip** /skɪp/ *v.* 蹦跳；略过；有意不出席；匆匆离开

☆ **halt** /hɔːlt/ *v.* 停止行进；终止

Two Cockroaches

趣味笑话

Two cockroaches were munching on garbage in an alley when one engages a discussion about a new restaurant.

"I was in that new restaurant across the street," said one. "It's so clean! The kitchen is spotless, and the floors are gleaming white. There is no dirt anywhere — it's so sanitary that the whole place shines."

" Please," said the other cockroach frowning. "Not while I'm eating!"

两只蟑螂

两只蟑螂正在一条胡同里的垃圾堆上大吃特吃，一只开始谈论一家新开张的餐厅。

"我去了街对面那家新餐厅，"它说，"那儿太干净了！厨房里一尘不染，地板洁白得闪闪发亮。哪儿都没有脏东西，那地方整洁卫生得都发光了。"

"够啦，够啦，"另一只蟑螂皱着眉头说，"不要在我吃饭的时候说！"

☆ **munch** /mʌntʃ/ *v.* 津津有味地嚼；出声咀嚼

☆ **cockroach** /ˈkɒkrəutʃ/ *n.*【昆】蟑螂

☆ **spotless** /ˈspɒtlɪs/ *a.* 极其清洁的；没有污点的

☆ **sanitary** /ˈsænɪtəri/ *a.* 公共卫生的；有益于健康的

动物趣闻

Questions and Answers

问与答

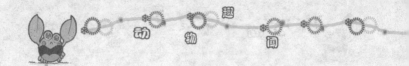
Questions and Answers

Q: What do you get when you cross an elephant with a kangaroo?

A: Holes all over Australia.

Q: What do you get if you cross an elephant with a whale?

A: A submarine with a built-in snorkel.

Q: Why do elephants have trunks?

A: Because they would look silly with glove compartments.

Q: Why do elephants drink so much?

A: To try to forget.

Q: What do you get when two giraffes collide?

A: A giraffic jam.

问 与 答

问：把大象和袋鼠杂交会怎么样？

答：澳大利亚到处都是坑。

问：把大象和鲸鱼杂交会产生什么？

答：自带水下通气管的潜水艇。

问：为什么大象长着长长的鼻子？

答：因为要它们带着储物箱看起来很傻。

问：大象为什么喝那么多？

答：借酒消愁。

问：两只长颈鹿撞在一起会发生什么事情？

答：长颈鹿堵塞。

☆ **cross** /krɒs/ *v.* 使杂交

☆ **submarine** /ˌsʌbməˈriːn/ *n.* 潜水艇

☆ **snorkel** /ˈsnɔːkəl/ *n.* （潜水艇的）水下通气管；（潜游者使用的）水下呼吸管

☆ **glove compartment** （汽车仪表板上存放手套等小物件用的）储物箱

Q: Which side of a chicken has the most feathers?

A: The outside.

Q: What do you get when you cross a parrot with a centipede?

A: A walkie-talkie, of course.

Q: Why don't they play poker in the jungle?

A: Too many cheetahs.

Q: What is the difference between a cat and a comma?

A: One has the paws before the claws and the other has the clause before the pause.

Q: Where do dogs go when they lose their tails?

A: To the retail store.

问：小鸡的哪一面长的毛最多？

答：外面。

问：把鹦鹉和蜈蚣杂交会产生什么？

答：当然是步话机喽。

问：为什么不在丛林里打牌？

答：猎豹太多了。

问：一只猫和一个逗号有什么不同？

答：猫先长脚掌后长出利爪；逗号停顿的前面有从句。

问：狗的尾巴丢了会去哪儿？

答：去零售店。

☆ **centipede** /'sentɪpi:d/ *n*. 蜈蚣，马陆

☆ **paws→pause** / **claws→clause**

☆ **tail** /teɪl/ *n*. 尾巴　　**retail** /'ri:teɪl/ *n*. 零售

Q: Why do hummingbirds hum?

A: Because they don't know the words.

Q: Where does a blackbird go for a drink?

A: To a crow bar.

Q: Why was the crow perched on a telephone wire?

A: He was going to make a long-distance caw.

Q: Why do hens lay eggs?

A: If they dropped them, they'd break.

Q: Why do seagulls live near the sea?

A: Because if they lived near the bay, they would be called bagels.

Q: Why did the turtle cross the road?

A: To get to the Shell station!

问：蜂鸟为什么嗡嗡叫？

答：因为它们不知道怎么说。

问：黑鸟去哪儿喝水？

答：去乌鸦吧。

问：乌鸦为什么落在电话线上？

答：它要打长途。

问：母鸡为什么下蛋（放下蛋）？

答：因为如果把蛋掉下来，蛋就会碎了。

问：为什么海鸥在近海的地方飞？

答：因为它们要是在海湾附近飞，就要被叫作"硬面包圈"了。

问：乌龟为什么要过马路？

答：到龟壳站（加油站）去。

Q: Why do birds fly South?

A: Because it's too far to walk.

Q: How to catch a polar bear?

A: Go up north and find a frozen lake or pond. Cut a large hole in the ice. Open a can of green peas, and place the peas around the edge of the hole single file. Hide behind a nearby rock. When the bear comes up to take a pea, kick him in the ice-hole!

Q: What is the greatest worldwide use of cowhide?

A: To cover cows, of course!

问：为什么鸟们要飞去南方？

答：因为要走着去太远了。

问：怎样抓到一只北极熊？

答：到北方去，找一个结了冰的湖或池塘。在冰面上凿一个大洞。开一罐嫩豌豆，把豌豆沿着洞口摆一排。然后藏在附近的岩石后面。等北极熊出来拿豌豆吃时，一脚把它踢进冰洞里！

问：全世界通用的母牛皮的最大的用途是什么？

答：当然是罩在母牛身上了！

☆ **hummingbird** /'hʌmɪŋbɜːd/ *n.*【鸟】蜂鸟

☆ **hum** /hʌm/ *v.* 发连续低沉的声音（如蜜蜂、马达等的嗡嗡声）

☆ **caw** /kɔː/ *n.* 鸦叫声（caw→call）

☆ **lay** /leɪ/ *v.* 产卵，下蛋；搁置，放下

☆ **sea→seagull / bay→bagel**

☆ **shell** /ʃel/ *n.*（软体动物或龟的）壳质；壳料
　　Shell 壳牌，一家全球化的综合型能源公司，勘探、生产并炼制石油，开发天然气资源等。